RESCUING THE WHALE

by John McInnes *Illustrated by*  *...a Denti*

E A R L Y   B I R D   C O L L E C T I O N   A U T H O R S

John McInnes, *Senior Author*   Glen Dixon   John Ryckman

All summer long the whales lived
in the cold waters of the Arctic Ocean.
There was plenty of food
for them to eat.

Summer ended and the days grew colder.
The ocean began to freeze over.
Sometimes the whales had to
break through thin ice
to make breathing holes.

It was time for the whales to head for warmer waters.

Most of the whales
began their journey south.
But three California gray whales
didn't leave soon enough.
Suddenly it got very cold.

An Inuit saw the whales and knew they were in danger.

He raced back to his village
and told the others what he had seen.
They all wanted to help rescue the whales.

The Inuit people hurried
to where the whales were trapped.
They chopped at the ice
to keep the breathing holes open.

A scientist made a videotape of what was happening. He sent it to a TV station.

People all over the world
heard about the whales.
They wanted to help rescue them.
They sent helicopters with special equipment.

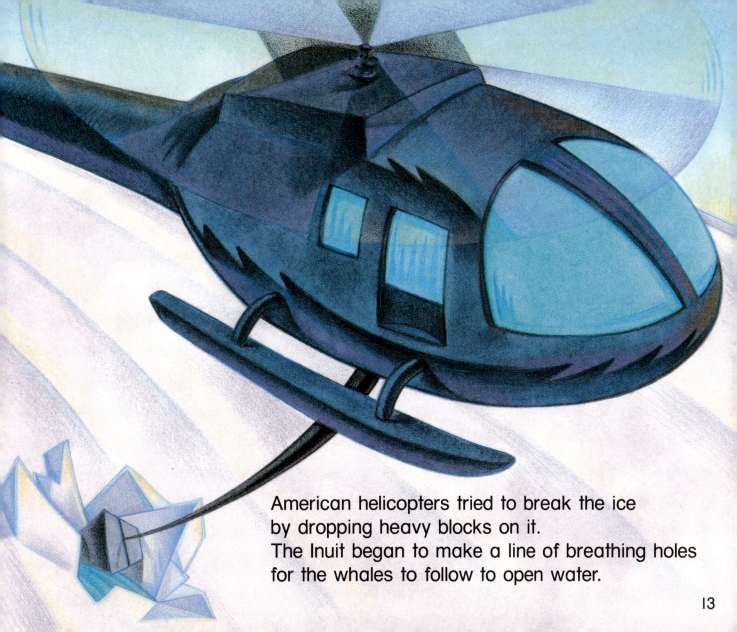

American helicopters tried to break the ice by dropping heavy blocks on it.
The Inuit began to make a line of breathing holes for the whales to follow to open water.

Meanwhile, the three whales
were getting weaker and weaker.
After awhile, only two of them surfaced.
The littlest one was never seen again.

After two weeks, a Russian ice-breaker
smashed its way through the ice.
Soon a wide channel had been cleared.

The two whales followed the ice-breaker to the open sea. At last they were free.

PUBLISHED SIMULTANEOUSLY IN 1990 BY:

Nelson Canada,
A Division of Thomson
Canada Limited
1120 Birchmount Road
Scarborough, Ontario M1K 5G4

AND

Delmar Publishers Inc.,
A Division of Thomson Corp.
2 Computer Drive, West
Box 15015
Albany, NY 12212-5015

**Canadian Cataloguing
in Publication Data**

McInnes, John, 1927-
  Rescuing the whales

(Early bird collection)
ISBN 0-17-603116-2

1. Whales - Juvenile literature. 2. Wildlife rescue - Juvenile literature. I. Denti, Suzanne. II. Title. III. Series.

QL737.C4M35 1990   j599.5   C90-093208-2

**Library of Congress
Cataloging-in-Publication Data**

McInnes, John, 1927-
  Rescuing the whales / by John McInnes ; illustrations by Suzanne Denti.
    p. cm.—(Early bird)
    Summary: Relates how a team of workers drilled holes in the frozen Arctic Ocean to save the lives of three whales and lead them to warmer waters.
    ISBN 0-8273-4164-4
    1. Gray whale—Alaska—Juvenile literature. 2. Wildlife—Alaska—Juvenile literature. [1. Whales. 2. Wildlife rescue.] I. Denti, Suzanne, ill. II. Title. III. Series: Early bird (Albany, N.Y.)
QL737-C425M37 1990
639.9'7951—dc20   89-71541
                                                    CIP
                                                    AC

© Nelson Canada,
A Division of Thomson Canada Limited, 1990

All rights in this book are reserved.

Co-ordinating Editor: Jean Stinson
Project Managers: Jocelyn Van Huyse-Wilson/Norma Kennedy
Editors: Irene Cox/Lisa Collins
Art Director: Lorraine Tuson
Series Design and Art Direction: Rob McPhail
Typesetting: Nelson Canada

1 2 3 4 5 6 7 8 9 0 EB 9 8 7 6 5 4 3 2 1 0